STORIES

AND

SONGS

STORIES

AND

SONGS

The Scriptural Application of
Blessed Assurance

A Book of Encouragement, Hope,
Praise, and Worship

Elton F Chesser

STORIES AND SONGS
The Scriptural Application of Blessed Assurance

Elton F. Chesser

Scripture quotations are from the King James Version of the Bible.

Printed in the United States of America

ISBN 978-1-961482-12-8

TABLE OF CONTENTS

Dedication

Dedicated to the memory of my mother, Eunice J. Chesser, who introduced me to the unfailing love of Christ and the power of the Holy Spirit. Her love was completely unconditional.

Acknowledgments

Special thanks to all who shared their stories for this book. Editing your stories brought tears of pain for the struggles you experienced, and tears of joy for the grace, love, mercy, and power of the Holy Ghost you found.

PREFACE

I was sitting in an Assisted Living Facility with a few of the members of my church singing hymns with the residents. Nothing out of the ordinary. At the time, we were singing at three different facilities each month to bring a little old-time worship to them. We would always sing the old hymns they know and love.

One day in particular, we were singing "Blessed Assurance." I'm sure I've sung this old hymn hundreds of times in my life, beginning at the church where I grew up in Harvey, Illinois. As we were singing, suddenly this song began to affect me like never before. I allowed the words to soak into my heart and mind. I realized, I suppose for the first time, every single line and phrase of this song leaped right off the pages of God's Holy Word.

In the next few days, I began to read the lyrics of "Blessed Assurance" and search for the relating Scripture. Before my very eyes, I saw stacks of Scripture which represented every line Fanny J. Crosby had written.

Since that day, I have been honored to preach from the pulpit, the song and message, "Blessed Assurance." As I present to you, in this book, the lyrics of "Blessed Assurance" and the corresponding Scripture, I trust it will bless your soul the way it did mine as I sang it in that Assisted Living Facility.

Sincerely,
Elton F. Chesser

Section One

THE SONG

The Author

Fanny J. Crosby

On the 24th day of March 1820 in New York State, a baby was born to John and Mercy Crosby. They named their baby girl Frances Jane Crosby, but over the next decades and beyond, she would become known as Fanny.

If you've ever held an old church hymn book in your hands you've no doubt noticed her name printed on the pages of some popular and well-known hymns. Hymns such as, "Close to Thee," "I am Thine O Lord," "Pass Me Not O Gentle Saviour," and "Praise Him Praise Him," to name a few.

When Fanny was just six weeks old, she developed an infection in her eyes. Her concerned parents made a call to a local physician who, recognizing the infection, devised a plan for healing. The doctor placed hot poultices on the baby's eyelids. While the infection did eventually go away, the treatment left scarring on Fanny's eyes, which caused her to lose her eyesight. She would spend the rest of her life blind.

Months later, Fanny's father would fall ill and pass, leaving Mercy Crosby a widow at twenty-one years of age, with a blind infant to care for. John Crosby's mother, Eunice, stepped up to help Mercy and care for Fanny as her mother began working as a maid.

Grandmother Eunice Crosby took caring for Fanny very seriously. She would describe to Fanny the beauty of the world, read the Bible to her, and emphasize the importance of prayer.

As a teen, Fanny enrolled in the New York Institute for the Blind and later became a teacher. She taught rhetoric and history for more than two decades, while writing poems and songs. Fanny would eventually marry Alexander van Alstine, a musician and former student of the institute.

In 1873, while Fanny was visiting one of her friends, Composer Phoebe Palmer Knapp, Knapp sat at the piano and played a melody she had recently written. Knapp asked Fanny what she thought the melody was saying. "Blessed Assurance, Jesus is Mine," Fanny responded. The two would sit together playing melody and adding lyrics and would compose the song we know today as "Blessed Assurance."

In their lifetimes, Knapp would compose more than five hundred songs and Fanny J. Crosby would write lyrics for more than eight thousand hymns. Fanny was writing so many hymns that her publisher insisted she begin writing under a pseudonym to prevent the public from thinking they only published Fanny J. Crosby songs.

During her lifetime, Fanny J. Crosby was able

to develop relationships with several presidents, including Martin Van Buren, John Tyler, James K. Polk, and Grover Cleveland. She also once addressed the U.S. Senate and later, a joint session of Congress concerning the subject of education for the blind.

Francis Jane Crosby van Alstine died February 12, 1915, of a cerebral hemorrhage following a six-month illness. She was five weeks and five days shy of her 95th birthday. Fanny is buried in Mountain Grove Cemetery in Bridgeport, CT, near her mother and other relatives.

"How many blessings I enjoy that other people don't. To weep and sigh because I am blind, I cannot, and I won't."

Fanny J. Crosby

Blessed Assurance

Verse One

Blessed Assurance, Jesus is mine....

> A man that hath friends must shew himself friendly: And there is a friend that sticketh closer than a brother.
>
> Proverbs 18:24

Seems to be a simple concept. If you want to have friends, you must be friendly, or rather, you must be a friend to others. The depth of a friend varies depending upon the friend. Perhaps the depth of any friendship is defined by how faithful, or dedicated the friend might be, and how faithful and dedicated one is to the friendship.

I have had many people in my life who I might consider to be a friend, but the depth of intimacy and closeness held within the relationship greatly depended upon how deep my trust in that person would lie.

Then there's convenience. Some friendships fade away because someone moves to live elsewhere and contact is eventually lost. We don't see them as often or have an opportunity to speak with them as often. Or maybe we just don't take the time. Not all friendships are convenient; however, if they are important to us, we make sure they last.

No doubt every one of us has at one time or another been hurt by someone we thought was a trusted friend. If we think about it, their name, and what they did to hurt us, still hide in the deepest shadows of our memory, even if we did long ago forgive them.

But there's a beautiful part to this Proverb as well: "… there is a friend that sticks closer than even a brother." That's pretty close!

Many of us have had that one friend who we have no idea how life would have been without them. When good things happen, they're the one person we call. When bad things happen, again, they are the one person we call. That's the person we would trust with our lives ten times out of ten. They seem to always be there when we need them. Without fail. Kinda sounds like Jesus, doesn't it?

Here's the beautiful thing about being a true child of God: He's always there. In good times, He's there. In bad times, He's there. When life is near perfect, He's there. When we stumble and fail, He's there. He sticks with us through thick and thin. He's the one we can go to no matter the circumstance. When we dedicate our lives to Him, He's got us, because He has already dedicated His life to us. It doesn't get any better than that. He's with us until the end of the world.

Blessed Assurance... Jesus is mine. He's all mine.

Oh, what a foretaste of glory divine....

> Beloved now are we the sons of God, and it
> doth not yet appear what we shall be: but we
> know that, when he shall appear, we shall be
> like him; for we shall see him as he is.
>
> I John 3:2

Have you ever gone out to eat in a nice restaurant and, when you walk inside the doorway, you can already smell the amazing food you're about to order and eat? So it is with living an overcoming life in Christ. Visitors walk into a Spirit-filled church for the first time and can feel something they have never felt in denominational churches.

I have had people tell me, while sitting in a church service they began to weep and cry, but they didn't understand why. You're feeling a foretaste of Glory Divine.

I've seen repentant people at the altar testify that they felt victory in their spirit. They felt forgiveness. Feel the glory.

People who receive the Holy Ghost with the evidence of speaking in tongues for the very first time, find themselves responding and acting in a way (in church) that they've never acted before. They're feeling glory. It's a foretaste of what will come.

"O taste and see that the Lord is good: Blessed is the

man that trusteth in him" (Psalm 34:8).

Taste and see...you won't be disappointed!

If you find yourself struggling with areas of life, give the Lord an opportunity to help you. If you need to trust Him more, or find forgiveness for unrepented sin, give it to Him. It will be a taste of Who He is, and He won't disappoint. As a matter of fact, Psalms tells us if we'll trust in Him, we'll be blessed. Wouldn't you rather put your trust in the Lord than in the darkness of this world?

> Behold, I shew you a mystery: We shall not all sleep, but we shall all be changed, in a moment, in the twinkling of an eye, at the last trump: for the trumpet shall sound, and the dead shall be raised incorruptible, and we shall be changed. For this corruptible must put on incorruption, and this mortal must put on immortality. So, when this corruptible shall have put on incorruption, and this mortal shall have put on immortality, then shall be brought to pass the saying that is written, Death is swallowed up in victory. O death, where is thy sting? O grave, where is thy victory?
>
> I Corinthians 15:51-59

One of my favorite Scriptures. Apostle Paul wrote this passage in his first letter to the church in Corinth. He wanted us to understand this mystery of "change." Our mortal self shall put on immortality. Death will never again sting, and the grave will never again have victory over us.

When you are in a Spirit-filled church service, in a prayer meeting, or even at home alone praying and worshiping the Lord, what you are feeling is that foretaste of the glory that is to come. A little bit of Heaven that Jesus allows us to feel now.

Can you imagine a life without pain? No more achy joints, no more contacts or reading glasses. No more canes or wheelchairs. No more doctor appointments, and no more death. Oh, what a foretaste of Glory Divine!

Heir of salvation....

> But when the fulness of the time was come, God sent forth his Son, made of a woman, made under the law, to redeem them that were under the law, that we might receive the adoption of sons. And because ye are sons, God hath sent forth the Spirit of his Son into your hearts, crying, Abba, Father. Wherefore thou art no more a servant, but a son; and if a son, then an heir of God through Christ.
> Galatians 4:4-7

When we come to the Lord seeking Him, we typically desire to be His servant. That's a good thing. We should live a life desiring to follow the Father's will at all times. But Apostle Paul makes it clear, at some point we leave the position of servant (although we should always seek to serve), and we become a son. And if a son, an heir. How do we know we are an heir of salvation? An heir of God? Verse six tells us He sends His Spirit into our hearts.

In the Church of the Lord Jesus Christ, one does not "join." No church roll, pastor's handshake, nor sinner's prayer will make you a family member. You must be born into this family. It happens when you are born of His Spirit. Then you become an heir. He is your Father, Abba, Daddy. It's an intimate relationship. He has your heart, and you have His salvation.

> For as many as are led by the Spirit of God, they are the sons of God. For ye have not received the spirit of bondage again to fear; but ye have received the Spirit of adoption, whereby we cry, Abba, Father. The Spirit itself beareth witness with our spirit, that we are the children of God.
>
> Romans 8:14-16

If you are filled with the power of the Holy Spirit, you have not received the spirit of fear. You need to realize you are a child of the Most High God. Your spirit bears witness, or agrees, with the Spirit of the Holy Ghost, that you are His child. He has adopted you or chosen you. You are born of God because He chose you to be His child. Rejoice that you are an heir of His salvation and all He has to give to you.

Purchase of God....

> What? Know ye not that your body is the temple of the Holy Ghost which is in you, which ye have of God, and ye are not your

own? For ye are bought with a price: therefore, glorify God in your body, and in your spirit, which are God's.

I Corinthians 6:19,20

Let's start with "ye are bought with a price." This statement within itself could fill volumes of books. The price Jesus paid to purchase you, to save you, and redeem you....

First of all, Jesus was betrayed by one of His very own. The "religious leaders" condemned Him and even paid people to lie against Him in their testimonies. Jesus was stripped naked, beaten, mocked, slapped, spit upon, and had a crown of thorns smashed into his head and brow. Roman solders drove stake-like nails through His wrists and feet, fixing Him to the cross.

While hanging on the cross, for crimes which He did not commit, onlookers shouted at Him with insults and jeers. His robe, which had been stolen from Him, was gambled off to a stranger. Even one of the thieves who was crucified at the same time, challenged His power.

Finally, about three o'clock in the afternoon, after hanging on the cross for a number of hours, He gave up the ghost. He bled out. All the blood in His body drained from Him, leaving Him lifeless. Jesus literally shed all His blood for you and for me.

Up to that point, it was a lamb who shed its blood and died, rolling the sins of Israel forward for one year, until it had to be done all over again. But Jesus died for you, shedding His blood for you once and for all. The writer of Hebrews said it this way, "... we are sanctified through the offering of the body of Jesus Christ once for all" (Hebrews 10:10). You are indeed purchased of God through the shed blood of His Son Jesus Christ.

Now let's talk about that body of yours. You are not your own, since Jesus paid a price for you. The Apostle Paul instructs us that our bodies are the temple of the Holy Ghost.

To the religious Jew, the temple was a very sacred place. It was a holy place reserved for prayer, praise, and worship to the Most High God.

Jesus Himself became angry because the money changers had devised a plan to earn income from sacrifices, and they set up shop right there in the temple. Jesus, chasing them out with a whip while overturning their tables, accused them of turning God's house into a den of thieves.

When Paul stated that our bodies were the "temple" of the Holy Ghost, he was not stating it lightly. It was a serious matter to Apostle Paul. Just as the physical Jewish temple was to remain holy, so also our bodies are to remain holy. He purchased us, so we are not our own.

I'll spare you the pages and pages of teaching concerning things which defile the body and instruction on how to keep yourself holy. I will say, a good start is a desire to know Jesus more and more.

If we seek Him and His perfect will, He will lead us into all truth.

Born of His Spirit....

> Jesus answered, Verily, verily, I say unto thee, except a man be born of water and of the Spirit, he cannot enter into the kingdom of God. That which is born of the flesh is flesh; and that which is born of the Spirit is spirit"
>
> John 3:5-6

Born of His Spirit. I love that. Shall we go straight to Acts Chapter 2?

> And when the day of Pentecost was fully come, they were all with one accord in one place. And suddenly there came a sound from Heaven as of a rushing mighty wind, and it filled all the house where they were sitting. And there appeared unto them cloven tongues like as of fire, and it sat upon each of them. And they were all filled with the Holy Ghost, and began to speak with other tongues, as the Spirit gave them utterance.
>
> Acts 2:1-4

This is exactly what Jesus was talking about when he was teaching Nicodemus, in John chapter three. He told his disciples, before He ascended into Heaven, that believers would speak with new tongues. Then breathing upon them, He instructed them to receive the Holy Ghost. "And when he had said this, he breathed on them, and saith unto them, Receive ye the Holy Ghost" (John 20:22).

When we do receive the Spirit of the Holy Ghost and speak in tongues, we are assuredly born of His Spirit. And may I add, it is still for all people today.

Washed in His blood....

> ... but now in Christ Jesus ye who sometimes were far off are made nigh by the blood of Christ.
>
> Ephesians 2:13

> But if we walk in the light as He is in the light, we have fellowship one with another, and the blood of Jesus Christ His Son cleanses us from all sin.
>
> I John 1:7

The priests of Israel stayed busy sacrificing bullocks, rams, lambs, and other animals attempting to keep Israel holy. "For it is not possible that the blood of bulls and of goats should take away sins" (Hebrews 10:4).

The blood of animals only washed their sins and offenses ahead for a season, never completely washing them all away. It was the blood of Christ the Messiah that fully washed sins away once and for all. "And they overcame him by the blood of the lamb, and by the word of their testimony, and they loved not their lives unto the death" (Revelation 12:11).

Let's take a moment to analyze verse 11 of Revelation chapter 12. John notes three things which allowed some to overcome the evil of the enemy and the darkness of the world.

The first was that they overcame by the blood of the Lamb, who we know to be Jesus. His blood is the only thing that can wash us clean from our sin to guarantee heaven. Without the blood of Christ shed upon us, we would have no hope for eternity.

Secondly, John mentioned the "word" of their testimony. In other words, they spoke it out. They were not fearful to proclaim what Jesus had done for them. This is part of the reason for the writing of this book. You need to proclaim to others what Christ has done for you. We were lost and undone, hopeless and helpless, until Christ.

I pray the testimonies, in a later section of this book, move you and encourage you to speak up and speak out to others of what the Lord has done for you.

And lastly, John tells us these folks loved Jesus and their life in Him more than their own lives. They were literally willing to die for their testimony and love for Jesus.

> And one of the elders answered, saying unto me, What are these which are arrayed in white robes and whence came they? And I said unto him, Sir, thou knowest. And he said to me, These are they which came out of great tribulation, and have washed their robes, and made them white in the blood of the Lamb. Therefore are they before the throne of God,

and serve Him day and night in His temple; and he that sitteth on the throne shall dwell among them. They shall hunger no more, neither thirst any more; neither shall the sun light on them, nor any heat. For the Lamb which is in the midst of the throne shall feed them, and shall lead them unto living fountains of waters; and God shall wipe away all tears from their eyes.

Revelation 7:13-17

I want you to realize how important it is to be washed in the blood of the Lamb, and what a change it makes for your eternity. Apostle John saw these, who gathered with the angels and elders, around the throne worshiping the Lamb. They were there because they had been washed in the blood of the Lamb. Now in Heaven, after coming out of the great tribulation, they will hunger no more, neither thirst anymore, nor be burned with the sun ever again. But they will be fed and live among living fountains of water with the Lamb.

Blessed Assurance

Verse Two

Perfect Submission....

> "Submit yourselves therefore to God. Resist
> the devil, and he will flee from you.
>
> James 4:7

Often the thought of submission seems so awful and demeaning. It's sometimes difficult to submit to an arrogant boss or supervisor. Whenever we deal with someone of authority, perhaps we cringe at the thought of submitting to them. But, submission to the Lord serves a number of purposes.

First of all, to submit to the Lord grants us the ability to submit to His will. When we submit to the will of God, we are resting in His care. Granted, the "will" of God may not always be a comfortable place. Ask Jacob's son, Joseph. But by submitting to God and His will, even if He takes us through an uncomfortable valley, we know we are well taken care of.

Secondly, just as James wrote in his letter, by submitting to God, it gives us the strength to resist the devil, which will in turn cause Satan to flee from us. Why do we fear the enemy? Why do we wrestle with life? The enemy will flee from you if you submit yourself to God and resist the devil. I would call that perfect submission.

"Trust in the Lord with all thine heart; and lean not unto thine own understanding. In all thy ways acknowledge him, and he shall direct thy paths" (Proverbs 3:5-6).

You must trust to be able to submit, and when you trust the Lord with all your heart, that is total submission.

Perfect Delight....

> Delight thyself also in the Lord; And he shall give thee the desires of thine heart.
>
> Psalm 37:4

Ok, here's one we may have to fake occasionally. When the bills are due and there's more bills than money, it's difficult to be delighted. When our kids, grandkids, or we ourselves are sick in bed running a fever, it's difficult to be delighted. But there is a principle in the Word of God, and life in general, that teaches us a positive attitude, and an upbeat mindset will raise us above the doldrums.

So, even when life is not being very kind to us, let us delight ourselves in the Lord. Perhaps we may not be able to delight in the negative things that occasionally occur. But let's think of good things. Let us delight ourselves in the wonders of God. Let us delight ourselves in the fact that we are His and He is ours. The fact that He loves us so much, He was willing to give Himself up for our salvation. After all, He has built a mansion for us if we accept it. Perfect delight! "Finally, brethren, whatsoever things are true, whatsoever things are honest, whatsoever things are just, whatsoever things are pure, whatsoever things are lovely, whatsoever things are of good report; if there be any virtue, and if there be any praise, think on these things" (Philippians 4:8).

A great part of delight is mindset. Folks who are constantly looking for a problem, or something to complain about, are rarely happy. Might I add, I believe it's usually their own fault.

Now I'm not saying we should ignore problems or challenges and pretend life is perfect. If we think like that, we'll soon lose our homes for non-payment and our health by ignoring what doctors call "warning signs." We do need to take care of the business side of life. But let us not "live there."

There's a lot about life to rejoice in and be glad about. There are things in our lives that never fail to make us smile or give us the "feel goods."

My precious mother lived to be eighty-seven years old. She dealt with cardiac issues much of her life, and later constantly teetered on the edge of needing to begin dialysis. I would check on her and at times find her teary eyed and appearing to be discouraged. I would say, "Mom, what's going on?" She would say, "I'm just having a pity party." Mom got so tired of not feeling well.

I would tell her, "Mom, it's ok to have a pity party every now and then. I certainly understand how awful it must be to never really feel well." But then I would encourage her, "At some point you must shake it off and move on from the pity party. You can't live there. Remember the wonderful life the Lord blessed you with. Remember His saving grace and all the healings received. We certainly have a lot to praise Him for."

Some may disagree with me about the occasional pity party. Life isn't always nice to us. But through His love and grace we shake it off and give Him praise. In Him we can find perfect delight.

Visions of rapture now burst on my sight....

> ... looking for that blessed hope, and the glorious appearing of the great God and our Saviour Jesus Christ; who gave himself for us, that he might redeem us from all iniquity, and purify unto himself a peculiar people, zealous of good works.
>
> Titus 2:13,14

I remember as a child, I always enjoyed Independence Day. It really wasn't for the freedom I enjoyed, although my little heart was thankful for all I had. I was much too little to understand how our forefathers dredged out freedom for some little kid that would be born two centuries later. No, I loved those fireworks! Still do, as a matter of fact.

The explosions, the big booms, the colors. The various types of reports exploding in the skies above. In those moments, I wasn't considering the men who gave themselves on a battlefield so those who would live on could enjoy some semblance of freedom. I was simply enjoying the rapture.

As a child of God, one of our most longed for events is when Christ shall appear in the clouds to take us home. The sound of a trumpet, the dead rising before us, we who are alive and remain joining them in the skies.

When we think of the catching away of the bride of Christ, maybe we don't think about the blood shed at Calvary. The thorns in His brow, or the stripes upon His back. Yes, He took all that for us, so we could one day enjoy the fireworks...the rapture, if you will.

We need to have a vision of rapture. The hope of glory. Visions of rapture... the glorious appearing of the great God and our Savior, Jesus Christ.

> For the Lord himself shall descend from heaven with a shout, with the voice of the archangel, and with the trump of God: and the dead in Christ shall rise first: then we which are alive and remain shall be caught up together with them in the clouds, to meet the Lord in the air: and so shall we ever be with the Lord. Wherefore comfort one another with these words.
>
> I Thessalonians 4:16-18

I believe there should be great anticipation in each of us who have been redeemed and filled with the power of the Holy Ghost. Visions of rapture bursting in our souls, like bright fireworks exploding in the night sky on the evening of Independence Day.

"Looking for that blessed hope and the glorious appearing of the great God and our Saviour Jesus Christ" (Titus 2:13).

Angels descending bring from above....

> But to which of the angels said he at any time, Sit on my right hand, until I make thine enemies thy footstool? Are they not all ministering spirits, sent forth to minister for them who shall be heirs of salvation?
> Hebrews 1:13,14

Did you know, one of the purposes of the angels is to minister to the children of God? We are surrounded by angels at any given moment in time. They gather round about the people of God for protection. They minister peace. They bring blessings from above. They desire to have what we have in Christ. They are familiar with the very throne room of the Lamb. And we entertain them unaware.

"The angel of the Lord encampeth round about them that fear him, and delivereth them" (Psalm 34:7).

Can we make this personal? Did you know, if you are a child of God, and you fear (respect) the Lord, there's an angel or angels camped out around you at any given moment, sent to protect you or deliver you? See how important you are to the Lord?

I've never been one to go camping. Sleeping in a tent overnight with no running water or electricity just doesn't sound that appealing to me. Maybe I'm a little spoiled, ok? But there's an angel camped out near you, watching you, protecting you. They ascend and descend from the heavens, sent by God.

Echoes of Mercy....

> This I recall to my mind, Therefore have I hope. It is of the Lord's mercies that we are not consumed, because his compassions fail not. They are new every morning: Great is thy faithfulness.
>
> Lamentations 3:21-23

We should thank the Lord Jesus every day for His mercies which are made new every morning. Without His mercy we would be consumed. But, because He is a merciful God, we can have hope. Hope for a better life: one of forgiveness, love, grace and, yes, mercy.

Apostle Paul wrote in his first letter to the church in Corinth, that we are washed, sanctified, and justified in the name of the Lord Jesus, and by the Spirit of our God. Let us never take for granted the mercies of God. He is merciful because He has compassion and boundless love toward us.

"And such were some of you: but ye are washed, but ye are sanctified, but ye are justified in the name of the Lord Jesus, and by the Spirit of our God" (I Corinthians 6:11).

"The Lord is not slack concerning his promise, as some men count slackness; but is longsuffering to usward, not willing that any should perish, but that all should come to repentance" (II Peter 3:9).

In other words, the Lord will keep His promises. He is very patient with you, and it is not His will that you be lost. He desires for you to come to a place of repentance so He can forgive you. If that doesn't echo mercy, I don't know what does.

Whispers of love.... "For God so loved the world, that he gave his only begotten Son, that whosoever believeth in him should not perish, but have everlasting life" (John 3:16).

Stop reading for a moment and just think about how much He loves you. He loves you so much that He robed Himself in flesh, subjected Himself to the creation, took stripes upon His back to afford you healing, hung upon a cross in shame as a common criminal, and shed all the blood out of His body for your redemption. But even that wasn't the ending....

He rose from the dead the third day and poured out the power of the Holy Ghost on the day of Pentecost, and offered it to whosoever will, just so you could be saved from hell.

He loves you! Sometimes He whispers it, and sometimes He screams it. He loves you!

Every healing you've ever received is because He loves you. Every blessing you enjoy is because He loves you, and here's the icing on the cake...

"Precious in the sight of the Lord is the death of his saints" (Psalm 116:15).

He's looking forward to you being in Heaven with Him one day.

Blessed Assurance

Verse Three

Perfect submission....

> Humble yourselves therefore under the
> mighty hand of God, that he may exalt you in
> due time: casting all your care upon him; for
> he careth for you.
>
> I Peter 5:6

There's that nasty word again... submission! I suppose
Franny J. Crosby thought we needed to hear it twice.
It's really not a bad word when you think about who
you're submitting to.

By submitting to the Lord, yes, we submit our will.
We submit our desires, and we strive to have His
will become our will. But another part of submission
is giving Him all our cares and worries. All our
struggles, failures, disappointments, and goals. When
we submit, or cast our cares upon Him, it matters,
because it matters to Him.

Don't ever be afraid to submit yourself to the Lord.
The good, the bad, the hurt, all of it. When you submit
to Him, He is faithful to care for you.

All is at rest....

> Come unto me, all ye that labour and are heavy laden, and I will give you rest. Take my yoke upon you and learn of me; for I am meek and lowly in heart: and ye shall find rest unto your souls. For my yoke is easy, and my burden is light.
>
> Matthew 11:28-30

Perhaps rest is a reward for submission. Jesus is calling for you to come to Him and unload your heavy burden upon Him. Lay down the weight you've been carrying from the world and pick up His yoke. It's actually much lighter. Learn about Him, His compassion, His mercy, and love.

The weight of the world truly is a heavy burden to bear. Just ask the alcoholic, the drug addict, or the person who spent years wrecked by the desires of the world, who finally came to know the freeing power of Christ. They will testify the yoke, or burden of living for Jesus, is nowhere near the heaviness of sin.

One of the beautiful effects of living an overcoming life in Jesus Christ is a conscience cleansed of guilt and worry. You know what happens to someone with a clean conscience? They can rest.

> I have set the Lord always before me: Because he is at my right hand, I shall not be moved. Therefore, my heart is glad, and my glory rejoiceth: My flesh also shall rest in hope.
>
> Psalm 16:8-9

It's a spiritual chain reaction. When we set the Lord before us, make Him our right hand, and determine not to be moved by the cares of this life, it brings joy and gladness to our hearts. The joy and gladness bring rejoicing, which has a direct affect on our flesh, and we find rest.

Many times, our lack of rest, or the restlessness we find in our spirit, is because we have not fully given ourselves to the Lord. Give your heart to Him totally, without reserve and, even with the cares of this life, you'll find rest.

I in my Savior am happy and blest....

> Happy is the man that findeth wisdom, and
> the man that getteth understanding.
> Proverbs 3:13

Notice Fanny J. Crosby did not write, I, AND my Savior. She wrote, I, IN my Savior, am happy and blest. Our Savior is happy with or without us. He is a Sovereign God Who, to be painfully honest, doesn't need you or me, but He desires us. But oh, how we need Him.

It's truly amazing how someone battling depression and the angst of the world, can come to Jesus, be filled with His Spirit, and go home happy and joyous. Our financial situation may not have changed, our status, our job (or anything else) may not have changed but, when we are filled with His Spirit, we feel blessed.

You see, our soul sees and feels much more than our

carnal mind does. Our mind may want to dwell on the troubles, the shortcomings, and struggles. But when we live in Christ, our soul realizes there's so much more than simply this life. Our goal is the next life...the "spirit" one, when we hear a trumpet and we are called home. If we are IN our Savior and our Savior is IN us, we will feel happy and blessed.

Watching and waiting looking above....

> "Behold, I shew you a mystery; We shall not all sleep, but we shall all be changed, in a moment, in the twinkling of an eye, at the last trump: for the trumpet shall sound, and the dead shall be raised incorruptible, and we shall be changed. For this corruptible must put on incorruption, and this mortal must put on immortality. So when this corruptible shall have put on incorruption, and this mortal shall have put on immortality, then shall be brought to pass the saying that is written, Death is swallowed up in victory. O death, where is thy sting? O grave, where is thy victory?"
>
> I Corinthians 15:51-55

Oh, my goodness, this is one of my favorite Scriptures. I get excited reading it and thinking about it. Apostle Paul calls it a mystery but then explains it to us. We're going to change. We will finally be able to shed that heavy, worldly flesh that has caused us so much grief. Our corrupt flesh will be changed. Our mortality that we have wrestled with...going to see doctors and taking medications and the like...will be changed.

No more pain, arthritis, heart problems, death of loved ones, no more "expiration date." Death will be swallowed up. There will be no more sting, or pain in losing ones we love.

Fanny J. Crosby said, "We're watching and waiting, looking above." We're keeping our eyes on the eastern skies. As a child of God, let us live with great anticipation of the coming of the Lord. His return is going to change everything for His people, and we shall be with Him forever. "Looking for that blessed hope, and the glorious appearing of the great God and our Saviour Jesus Christ" (Titus 2:13).

Apostle Paul states, we should be looking for the coming of the Lord. We should live our lives for Christ, victoriously watching and waiting for that glorious day that is coming. We should live everyday with great anticipation of the sound of a trumpet, a shout and the appearing of our Lord and Saviour, Jesus Christ.

Filled with His goodness....

Rejoice in the Lord, O ye righteous: For praise is comely for the upright. Praise the Lord with harp: Sing unto him with the psaltery and an instrument of ten strings. Sing unto him a new song; Play skillfully with a loud noise. For the word of the Lord is right; And all his works are done in truth. He loveth righteousness and judgment: The earth is full of the goodness of the Lord.

Psalm 33:1-5

Here's a wonderful reason to rejoice in the Lord, praise Him, and sing unto Him with our hearts. That goodness of the Lord, that we feel deep inside, escapes into the world. We are the light for a dark world. Let us allow that light to flow from our rejoicing, praise, singing, and worship for all the world to see. Let's do our part so the world is filled with the goodness of God.

"But the fruit of the Spirit is love, joy, peace, longsuffering, gentleness, goodness, faith, meekness, temperance: against such there is no law" (Galatians 5:22-23).

If we are filled with His goodness, it will come out. Whatever things we feed our minds and hearts, it will show. This is what causes people, worshiping in a church service, to feel compelled to raise their hands or shout. When the Holy Ghost fills our spirit, we cannot help but lift our voices to worship Him.

There's another reaction as well, to being filled with the goodness of the Lord, which is the Fruit of the Spirit. If we are truly filled with His goodness, we will display the Fruit of the Spirit. Our lives will show that He is in our hearts. The life we live, the words we speak, and even our attitudes will show the goodness of the Lord.

Lost in His love....

Behold, what manner of love the Father hath bestowed upon us, that we should be called the sons of God: therefore the world knoweth us not, because it knew him not.

I John 3:1

These words take me back to times when we would meet for prayer, or simply not rush a church service, and let the Lord move in the way He desires. I have been in church services where the schedule of service basically comes to a stop because people are praying, crying, worshiping, and totally lost in His love.

It's during those prayer meetings and services that time stops. Our minds are allowed to leave this present world of schedules, jobs, duties, and the like, to simply bask in the love of Jesus. There are many distractions in this life, but let us never lose the desire to get lost in God's presence, or the ability to go deep into prayer. If you have ever gotten lost in the presence and love of Jesus, you don't want it to end.

Blessed Assurance

Chorus

This is my story, this is my song....

O Sing unto the Lord a new song Sing unto the Lord, all the earth, Sing unto the Lord, bless his name; Shew forth his salvation from day to day. Declare his glory among the heathen. For the Lord is great, and greatly to be praised: He is to be feared above all gods.

Psalm 96:1-4.

We all have a story. It's that part of our life that we may not always want to share, but it's part of what made us who we are. I have found those problems, struggles, and battles we may have faced, after we have come to know the Lord, becomes our greatest testimony.

Who better to guide the drug addict to the Lord other than someone who once was addicted and found deliverance? Who better to teach a grief class or encourage someone who just had a great loss in their life, than one who has been all too familiar with grief and, over time, found their way back to peace.

Apostle Paul, probably the greatest evangelist and

church builder the world has ever known, once referred to himself as the chiefest of sinners. Having once persecuted the church, and led some to death, now having found the revelation of Jesus Christ, traveled the known world of that day, saving souls from hell.

What is your story?

What is your defining moment?

Whatever it may be, if Jesus has led you to Him and has given you peace, I know you can look back and appreciate the journey. It has now become your testimony.

And coming to Christ, we find He gives us a new song. He changes our attitude, our thought process, and our desires. That's what the power of the Holy Ghost is for. To live in us and make us more like Jesus. Let us sing the new song He has given to us. A song of thanksgiving, of worship and of praise.

"Come and hear, all ye that fear God, and I will declare what he hath done for my soul" (Psalm 66:16).

In gathering testimonies for the last portion of this book, I asked some to share their stories who were very excited to share. Then there were those who hesitated or preferred not to share their stories with the public. I understand, the story of where Jesus brought you from, or how He directed your paths to do His perfect will, is a very personal thing.
But again, let me say, it is the most powerful word

you can share. You see, people may argue Scripture with you, but when you share your testimony with them, they can't deny what the Lord has done for you. I encourage you to share, as David, King of Israel wrote, "... I will declare what He hath done for my soul" (Psalms 66:16).

"And they overcame him by the blood of the Lamb, and by the word of their testimony; and they loved not their lives unto the death" (Revelation 12:11).

Praising my Saviour, all the day long...

> Praise ye the Lord. Praise God in his sanctuary: Praise him in the firmament of his power. Praise him for his mighty acts: Praise him according to his excellent greatness. Praise him with the sound of the trumpet: Praise him with the psaltery and harp. Praise him with the timbrel and dance. Praise him with stringed instruments and organs. Praise him upon the loud cymbals: Praise him upon the high-sounding cymbals. Let everything that hath breath Praise the Lord. Praise ye the Lord.
>
> Psalm 150:1-6

David, King of Israel, made it very clear, we should praise the Lord. How can we, thinking about where the Lord has brought us from, not praise Him?

Let the former addict praise Him. Let the former liar praise Him. Let the former adulterer praise Him. Let the former gossiper praise Him. Whomever we may be, and whatever our story may be, let us praise our Lord and Savior for giving us a new song. A song that came with mercy, grace, and forgiveness. Let us never take these gifts lightly. They came at a high price.

> Now unto the King eternal, immortal, invisible, the only wise God, be honour and glory for ever and ever. Amen.
>
> Timothy 1:17

Section Two

THESE ARE OUR STORIES

THIS IS MY STORY

Laura Butler-Knight
Kennett, Missouri

Looking back, I can see so many events leading me into the arms of the Lord. Being first generation Pentecostal, I was not raised in church at all. When I saw church buildings, I just thought that's where "old people" went before they died. I knew absolutely nothing about God. The only time I heard His name was when it was used in vain.

It was in middle school, playing basketball, that I met Rebecca. She was the "new girl" who just moved to town because her dad became the pastor of the local Baptist Church. She and I shared a love for the game of basketball and connected quickly on the court and became friends. I was a very short-tempered girl who loved to fight and get drunk. Along with that I cussed like a sailor.

God sent her and, through Rebecca, my journey to Him began.

Every day I would come home and pour whiskey in my pink Kool-Aid or PGA in my Hawaiian Punch, and drink until I went to bed. Soon that wasn't enough, and I would sneak the clear liquor to school. Every weekend I looked forward to a party to get drunk. This was my "peace" and my "freedom" from all the hurt and abuse I was experiencing at home. Those around me didn't know that this troubled, bad girl had hell locked inside of her and, when confronted, it was unleashed.

At nine years old, I locked eyes with my daddy as he lay in a puddle of his own blood dying of a shot gun wound. Soon afterward, I began looking forward to going to school because it was safer than home, and the basketball court was my sanctuary. Because behind closed doors I was being abused verbally, physically, and sexually by someone who was supposed to be a stepdad to me.

One day that would all change. Rebecca invited me to Sunday School with her. I had no idea what Sunday School was. I went and learned there was this God in Heaven and you talked to Him. He would save you.

I went home that night and after being abused yet again, I remember lying in my bed with tears streaming down my face looking up into a clear night sky full of stars and praying my very first prayer, "God if you are really up there, and you are really real, then send me a real dad".

The events that took place after this prayer were tragic and left me, my two younger sisters, and mom running for our lives. We left everything behind that day. I had just put supper on the table when my mother walked through the front door with blood on her face and clothing. Scared, she told us to hurry and grab some clothes and get in the car. After fleeing, and staying in motel after motel, we landed in a town that became home.

Fast forward...God answered that first prayer and sent me, "My Jerry," a stepdad who became my best friend. God answered my prayer. I still wasn't attending church, but I found my sanctuary again, the basketball court, which led me to another church where I was asked to play for their team in a tournament.

One night after practice I needed a ride back home to the next town, because my ride bailed on me. I recalled my aunt telling me they were visiting a church in that same town.

When I walked in and looked through the swinging double doors, I could not believe what I saw. A man doing cartwheels across the front of the church, people running in circles, others shouting and jumping. I stood there laughing and thought these people are crazy and I would never do this. The pastor walked back and invited me in, and I said, "No thanks, just here to get a ride from my aunt."

After this, the youth pastors sent me postcards inviting me to church and came by to say hi and invite me in person. I kept saying, no.

Every day after school I would go running in the neighborhood. One afternoon on my run I saw a couple that attended that crazy Pentecostal church, and they waved, and I stopped to be kind. They invited me over for a home Bible study and some of "Maw's homemade salsa." I agreed to it and told them I would let them know.

That night I went to bed and had a terrifying nightmare of Satan holding me in his lap and laughing. I woke, and that very day I ended up in a living room where I was given not only tons of salsa but "Into His Marvelous Light" Bible study. I did everything I said I would never do. That day I danced all over their living room. I never felt anything like it before. His love consumed me, and I began laughing in the Spirit and felt so much peace and joy.

I'll never forget it. It was February of 1999 when I received the Holy Ghost and was baptized in Jesus Name. I was sixteen years old then and now, twenty-four years later, I am still serving Him. He has become my everything.

THIS IS MY STORY

Gus Carcabasis
St. Rose, Louisiana

At the age of sixteen, I began smoking, drinking, and doing all types of drugs. All through those years (ten in all), God had His hand on me. There were many days and nights that I don't know how I got home or even remember what happened to me the night before.

I was taking uppers, downers, drinking, smoking… all in one night, and in very large quantities. I should have never lived but, by the Grace of God, He saw not what I was but what I could be!

On September 9, 1992, my life completely changed. It was a Wednesday night service, and the Pastor preached a message called, "Unsafe Life Boats."

God was moving in my life in a mighty way. He spoke to me and said, "If you take the first step toward the altar, I will carry you the rest of the way!" I finally gave in! I wanted the Holy Ghost more than anything else in my whole life, and as soon as I stood up and took one step toward the altar, God took over just as

He said He would. It felt like I was floating in mid-air. I guess you could say I felt like Peter when he walked on water. A supernatural experience.

When I reached the altar, I told God I would not leave until I received the gift of the Holy Ghost! Suddenly, I felt my body shaking by the power of God. My mouth began to chatter and then I was speaking in another language that I had never learned ... the evidence of the Holy Ghost! It was the most awesome experience!

Jesus reached down from Heaven, filled me with His Spirit, and in one night delivered me instantly from all drugs, alcohol, and cigarettes.... PRAISE GOD! From that moment, I dedicated my life to the Kingdom.

I pray that my story will touch the lives of others and give them encouragement to know, with the help and grace of God, you can do it, too!

"I can do all things through Christ which strengtheneth me" (Philippians 4:13).

(Note: Gus passed away suddenly on October 26, 2021. At the time of his passing, Gus had faithfully served God for twenty-nine years. He was a beloved husband, father, grandfather, and friend, as well as a member of his church's Board of Trustees, and a vital part of the music ministry).

THIS IS MY STORY

James Drain
Berkley, Michigan

My name is James Drain. I was blind until August 14, 2023, when I was healed by Jesus Christ.

I have had multiple sclerosis for many years. My first episodes happened about twenty years ago, when my feet went numb. Then I started having visual troubles about fifteen years ago. I worked in chemical factories for about twenty years, and several of those chemical factories primarily dealt with products made from methanol. Methanol alone can cause blindness.

About eight years ago my doctor told me I was so visually impaired that I should give up my license and stop driving and I should stop working in chemical factories. I did not.

My eyesight continued to deteriorate. The multiple sclerosis made me susceptible to deterioration, and the work with the chemicals exasperated the situation.

Then, about five years ago, it took a turn for the worse. I had to go to Neuro ophthalmologists to gather data and get pictures of my optic nerve, and they said there was very little of it left. What I had was a blind left eye and a right eye with what is called a fractured image. I had some small amount of imagery coming through, but none of it was in the correct place. It was like looking through a kaleidoscope at an incomplete image.

Until August 14, 2023... when Jesus healed me, and now I can see!

When I walked into church on August 14th, I had zero vision in my left eye and only 40% viable vision in my right eye. When I walked out of church that evening, I could see perfectly. I can see better than I was ever able to see before.

That night, I decided I needed to be baptized in Jesus' Name for several reasons. First, the Bible says that's what we are supposed to do. As disciples of Jesus Christ, we are to follow His instructions. My pastor and my church family has helped me to understand the Scriptures better. It's quite clear in there what we are supposed to do to follow Jesus and to be saved.

I was not asking for any healing. I wasn't thinking about it at all. I really was just giving my life to Jesus and letting Him do what He wanted with me. I really was just surrendering completely to Him. That is why I wanted to be baptized.

So, I got baptized and, when I came out of the water, I felt overjoyed. I spoke in tongues very briefly, and then the lights around me started to feel more intense than usual. I began to look around, and I could distinctly make out each of the lights, which was very strange because light was always hard for me to look at. It would just streak up whatever vision I did have and make me more blind than usual.

I could see the individual lights and, as I looked down, I saw the people in the crowd. I could never pick out individuals like that before, so I looked around, and I saw some faces, and I told the pastor, don't say anything yet. I was trying to make sure I was not imagining things. Then I looked past all the people and there was a row of flags along the back of the sanctuary, and I could make out each individual flag. I could see what flags they were, all the way to the back of the sanctuary.

Then I confirmed to the pastor, "Pastor, I really can... I can see." Everything since then has just been different. With my promise to Jesus, and His promise to me, I've been doing my best to bring in as many people as I can to be saved and, really, that's all I want to do with my time anymore.

I've said on a few different occasions through this process that this miracle wasn't meant for me. It's a miracle that happened to me, but this was meant to bring others. This was meant as a beacon for others to see, and come, and to learn to trust Jesus, too.

Jesus is doing wonders in this world, healing lots of people. The stories I've been getting, so many people. Jesus can heal you, too.

I hope the one thing that comes from this is that people will be brave in Jesus' Name and tell others what has happened to them.

My name is James Drain, and God healed my blindness.

THIS IS MY STORY

Victoria (Vicki) Galatas
Kenner, Louisiana

Looking back over my life, I can clearly see how God had His hand on me from the very beginning. The stories I could tell would reveal His hand in my life every step of the way.

Shortly after turning sixteen, I credit the Lord for allowing me to meet and marry an amazing young man, and by the time I was twenty-two, we had four children.

In times of despair and confusion, I would always turn to a Bible my mom had given me on my wedding day, trying to find clarity, peace, and purpose for my life. I'd pray, "God there has to be more to life than this!" Little did I understand, but Jesus was already at work on my behalf!

The Lord really began drawing me in the fall of 1978. My former brother in-law (though he was far from a Christian) kept telling me that I wasn't "saved" or going to heaven. In my way of thinking, there was no way God was going to send me to the same hell as a murderer or rapist! So, I made up my mind to read the Bible for myself and prove I wasn't a sinner.

My journey to find the answer started in October of 1978. As I read the Bible, the Lord began opening my eyes to the fact that I was absolutely not ready to go to heaven. From October 1978 to March of 1979, I had read my Bible (from cover to cover) six times, eagerly highlighting every detail of what God was showing me. When my husband would get home from work, I'd share each day's revelations with him.

The Lord quickly revealed to my husband and me our need to be baptized in Jesus' Name, and so began our search to find someone to baptize us in Jesus' Name. During this time, the charismatic movement was just beginning, and I thank the Lord every day He didn't allow that "confusion" to sidetrack us. Instead, Jesus continued to lovingly reveal the Truth, the whole Truth and nothing but the Truth!

We were eager to repent of our wrongs and quickly change anything in our lives that wasn't aligned with His Word. As the Word of God came alive in our lives, and as the Lord revealed life-changing Truths to us, we immediately did an about-face and allowed Him to change us as only He can.

We were "partiers" who went out nearly every weekend. We immediately stopped that! We stopped listening to music that didn't uplift the Lord in our lives! We stopped using foul language because we saw the truth that blessing and cursing cannot come out of the same fountain. We even stopped watching television because of the ungodly trash it was "feeding" into our minds. The Lord was showing us all these things (and a lot more), and because of His great mercy, we eagerly surrendered our lives to Him.

By February of 1979, we were convinced that no one truly believed the teachings of the Bible. We understood the importance of water baptism in Jesus' Name, and though we had researched various churches in our area, and had even attended some crusades in an effort to find someone who also believed in the importance of Jesus' Name Baptism (like the Bible says), it was all to no avail, so my husband decided to go on a fast.

About two weeks into the fast, my brother in-law had a medical event that he was sure he wouldn't survive, so, before going to the hospital, he had my sister call every church in the phone book asking if they baptized in Jesus' Name.

The replies she received was astounding, but suffice it to say, it was the very last church she called who gave us the answer we were looking for...the ONLY WAY they baptized was in Jesus' Name, and yes, they could baptize the four of us that very day!

Before baptizing us, the pastor talked with us. He was shocked to actually meet people who had repented to such a degree that they already had a keen understanding of the importance of Jesus' Name Baptism and living a holy life.

So, on March 13, 1979, we were baptized in Jesus'

Name. What a glorious moment it was, to come out of the water knowing, without a doubt, that our sins were washed away. Every wrong I had done in my life, gone!

The pastor asked us if we had been filled with the baptism of the Holy Ghost, to which we replied that we knew about the Holy Ghost but we didn't know we could actually have it! I'm thankful to say that on April 6, 1979, God gloriously filled me with the baptism of the Holy Ghost, with the evidence of speaking in other tongues!

Not only had my sins been washed away, but now I had the Power of God ... a power that would enable me to live an overcoming life for Jesus! I was no longer struggling to get through this life on my own. Jesus now lived in me, providing the power I would need!

I had made so many poor choices in my short life, but I could now see how Jesus used every one of my failures to bring me to Him ... what Grace ... what Mercy...what Love!

"This is my story ... this is my song ..." I'm gonna praise my Savior for all He has done to bring me joy and peace that truly passes all understanding!

THIS IS MY STORY

Lynette Green
Sullivan, Illinois

There was a time in my life when my family, ministry, home, and everything familiar would be turned upside down with unbearable uncertainty. This time in my life would be full of many choices, turns and trials but not without victory. My faith in God did not take away my pain, but I knew God would help me through whatever took place.

In 1994, God gave me a dream. He reached down into my life and changed me. I became a regular church goer and wanted to learn all I could about God. I started driving the church van in hopes to share the explosive joy I was feeling, that can only come from receiving the Holy Ghost. I was blessed and excited to serve the Lord.

On September 14,1996, I married Rocky Green. We had four beautiful children, Tyler, Sarah, Lacie, and Nathan. Even from childhood my dream in life had always been to be a mother and have a family. Now I could raise my children in a happy, God-centered home.

As our family grew, so did our ministries. Rocky, now called Brother Green, preached, taught Bible studies, and was the youth pastor. I drove the church van, taught Sunday school, and helped with fundraisers. We both were grateful God pulled us from this dark old world and gave us eternal life. We were willing to do all we could for the kingdom of God.

November 2003, we became pastors in Sullivan Illinois, with only nine voting members. We were excited about our new ministry and humbled God had chosen us for this field. In just a short time the church was filling up, and I was teaching Sunday school, doing fundraisers, and putting together ladies' activities. Brother Green was doing cell groups, outreach, Bible studies, and preaching his heart to anyone who would listen. We were very active in our community, and the church grew to around one hundred people. Our ministries were flourishing, our children were happy, and we were in a safe place financially, spiritually, and emotionally, but this would all change.

April 27, 2012, was the day that changed our lives forever. At 11 am the doctor entered the room where my husband Rocky, my mother, and I were sitting. He proceeded with the news Rocky had aggressive cancer, and it had spread to many parts of his body. As I sat paralyzed by what we heard, we waited in anticipation for the devastating news that would follow: he was terminal. The doctor told us he could live as long as ten years depending on how his body responded to treatment. Tears began to fall quickly from my eyes like bombs hitting the table. I was speechless.

On our drive back home, I sat in the back seat with my forehead pressed against the window. My thoughts were racing with what would the future hold? We had children who were too young to lose their dad. Our family would be broken. Tyler was only fourteen, Sarah twelve, Lacie eleven, and Nathan was only seven years old.

After a few weeks of crying and waking up in the middle of the night with night sweats and screaming, I tried to grasp my reality. We prayed for God to intervene. We prayed for a miracle. Chemo was started and Rocky was growing weaker. After time, my thoughts turned toward preparing for the harsh future ahead of us if God was going to take my husband home.

January 5, 2014, Rocky Green passed from this life. We had to move because we were in the church parsonage. The kids lost their dad and their home, church, school, community, and all the friends they had ever known. I lost my husband, ministry, home, income, basically everything. Now where do we go? Where did we belong?

With more than $30,000 in debt and only $10,000 in life insurance, financially, spiritually, and emotionally we needed God more now than ever. With debt and no where to go, nowhere to live and no direction, God was with us.

Financially, money came from every direction. Spiritually, I set my face like a flint toward heaven and God placed us right where we needed to be. Our emotional healing still continues.

Job feared the Lord and shunned evil. He had everything going for him until Satan came and wanted to try him. Trial after trial, Job did not sin or blame God. God's Word tells us his grief was very great, but he never turned away from God. He never lost his faith, and that's how I wanted to be.

When things settled, God gave me a beautiful home in Tennessee, all my debt was paid, He set us under one of the best pastors ever found, and gave us time to heal. The road was not always straight, and I know I made mistakes in my grief, but God was always there.

Today the earth-quaking tremble has settled as we try to rebuild. Our life will never be the same without Rocky Green (Dad), but life is what you make it, and we choose to make it our best life, because God gave it to us.

Currently, I own my own home in central Illinois and enjoy it with two of my children. We attend a wonderful Apostolic Church. My oldest son is married and is a minister of the gospel, and through my youngest daughter and her husband, I enjoy two grandchildren.

You can make it through the storm, just keep hanging on.

THIS IS MY STORY

Linda Mongeon
Manchester, Tennessee

"Linda, I'm not talking about a religion, I'm talking about a personal relationship with God." A personal relationship with God? I had never heard of any such thing! How could you possibly have an intimate relationship with God?

These were the words spoken to me by my brother, David, who was home on leave for Christmas from the Army. He had been born again a few months before at a Christian coffee house where he was stationed in Texas.

I was going through a very difficult time in my life, where every plan I had ever made was crumbling before me. I was bitter, broken-hearted, distrustful of everyone, and disillusioned with life. I was yearning deep within for that which I didn't know.

Two weeks later, on New Year's Eve, I found myself on my knees at an altar in a church that my brother's girlfriend attended, sobbing my heart out, knowing I would never be the same. You would think this would be the time I would give my whole life and heart to the Lord, but I had some deep-seated problems. I was unable to trust anyone, including God, and I wanted to be loved, thinking that would only come from a man.

I struggled with these problems for many years thereafter, until one day I realized I had come to the point where I had had enough. My way had only caused pain and suffering to my children and myself. That day, I totally surrendered to the Lordship of Jesus Christ in obedience to His will and His way.

In 2019, God began to really move in my life. In March of that year, I was given a ticket to a women's seminar by a friend who told me that the Lord had spoken to her that I was to go. Kathy Tricolli was the singer/speaker at the seminar. Kathy spoke two things that day that I knew were from the Lord for me.

The first was, "Take whatever you have covered up and let Him uncover it so He can heal you." I knew I was struggling with the shame and guilt of divorce and broken relationships. I had remarried my first husband who died eight years later. I chose that day to uncover that which I had covered up. It was painful to do so but was necessary to heal my shame and guilt. As women, we naturally seek after love. We were built that way, but until we give ourselves to the One Who IS love, we will never know genuine love.

In the fall of that year, I was told of a need for a volunteer at the hospice office where I lived. I am a retired RN. I had avoided working in oncology for the twenty-two years I was a nurse. I didn't think I could handle it emotionally. I knew finally that it wasn't about my feelings, it was about what they needed. So, I started volunteering.

That's when a God thing happened! The volunteer coordinator happened to be an Apostolic Pentecostal pastor. He asked me one day to attend a service at his church. I decided to go just one time. I went to that service and felt something happen deep down inside myself. The pastor asked me after service if I would consider coming to his church. I told him I would go home and pray about it, and if I felt the Lord in it, I would be back. After five days of almost non-stop prayer, I knew I was to go to that church. The words spoken was to go there and pour my life out and the culmination of all the things He had for me would be realized there. That was four and a half years ago, and He has been faithful.

The second thing Kathy spoke that day was, "Make me what you created me to be when you formed me in my mother's womb." The walls that I had spent years building up started to crumble and fall at that moment. The Lord started to return me to the person He had created me to be. I began to blossom under the care and love of the Lord, my pastor, and my brothers and sisters in the Lord.

I moved to Manchester, Tennessee, after a sermon called, "Come Follow Me," and was baptized in Jesus' Name, which totally changed my spiritual life. My life is wholly dedicated to the Lord, His kingdom, and His people.

Elton F. Chesser

He is real love. This is my story, this is my song, praising my Savior all the day long.

THIS IS MY STORY

Richard Mostyn
Houston, Texas

I was born the youngest of eight children into an Irish Catholic family in the city of Chicago. All eight of us attended Catholic schools all the way through high school. We were a devout Catholic family, and I was a dutiful altar boy in our neighborhood Catholic Church. Even with all of our church upbringing, we were still missing any spiritual connection.

My brother, who was a year older than me, moved to South Dakota looking to find some meaning in his life. He ended up living in a Catholic monastery among a group of monks, in the Black Hills of South Dakota. Still not finding what he was looking for, he made his way back to Chicago, to a little Pentecostal church which was only about a mile from where we grew up. We never even knew there was a Pentecostal church in our neighborhood and would not have known what it was even if we knew it was there.

My brother was introduced to Pentecost, and the oneness message, and baptism in Jesus' Name at Northside United Pentecostal Church, pastored by

71

Bobby Goddard. However, he did not receive the gift of the Holy Ghost, or the revelation of the great God in Christ, until he moved to the city of San Francisco, California.

There he was introduced to the Voice of Pentecost Church and Pastor Marilyn Gazowski. He was baptized in Jesus Name for the remission of his sins and received the Holy Ghost.

In July 1975, I decided to make my way to San Francisco to see my brother and become part of the hippie movement that was taking place in San Francisco. I went there with the intention of hanging out and getting high in this hippie utopia, but God had other plans.

My brother had invited me to stay with him in a home owned by Voice of Pentecost Church. It was one block from the corner of Haight and Ashbury, the epicenter of the hippie movement.

I thought I was in for some fun, but when I arrived, my brother informed me that, in order to stay in the home owned by the church, I had to attend church services. That was not my idea of a dream vacation, and as luck would have it, they were beginning their youth camp that next week, and there would be church every night.

I went to my first church service that Sunday, and it was a very shocking experience for this devout Catholic, former altar boy to take in. I thought these people had gone crazy. However, there was something very genuine about their worship, and I realized these people had experienced something that I had not, and needed, and didn't even know it.

By the third night of youth camp—and by camp, I mean camp—we were out in the woods in a beautiful area just over the Golden Gate Bridge, in a place that was called Kirby's Cove. We had set up tents and had sleeping bags, and it was a real camp. Church services were held in a clearing under some trees.

I can't even tell you what the preacher preached about the third night, but I sat on the ground holding onto a tree as if to anchor myself so I wouldn't make the mistake of going to the altar during the altar call. But something pulled me toward the altar, and I began to walk to the front. Before I knew it, I was in the spirit and hit the makeshift altar, sliding on my knees with tears pouring down my face.

God filled me that night with the gift of the Holy Ghost. The next morning, I was baptized in Jesus Name, in the Pacific Ocean with the Golden Gate Bridge in the background. My journey has taken many twists and turns since that day, but one thing I found out that week, those people had not lost their minds. They had found themselves, and they found the Lord.

I'm thankful every day for what happened that week, and I have not turned back to my old life since.

When that week was over, I headed back to Chicago, excited to tell everyone about my experience. I showed my mother my baptismal certificate, expecting her to be as excited for me as I was for myself. Instead, she told me to get that thing away from her. "You've already been baptized in the Catholic Church, and that's what counts." It was my first realization that not everyone is going to rejoice with me when I rejoice. But, regardless of what anyone else says or does, we must follow the leading of the Spirit and the Word of God above all else.

I went on to become the assistant pastor of a great church in Chicago, Illinois, under the pastorate of Elton F. Chesser. Later I moved to St Louis, Missouri, where I pastored for five years, before moving to Houston, Texas, to work alongside Pastor Michael Anderson at Christ Church Houston, where I remain to this day. I have failed many times, but God has never failed me once.

THIS IS MY STORY

James Oddo
New Orleans, Louisiana

After having spent twenty-two years in active ministry, eleven of which was spent traveling the world preaching the gospel, and eleven as senior pastor in Ruston, Louisiana, I made the decision to step away from ministry to try to preserve my family. The stresses of ministry had taken its toll on my marriage.

For eight years, I worked in senior management in the fields of construction logistics and oil and gas. As is inevitably the case, spiritual misalignment took its toll on my family and my life. My directional drilling business had gone bankrupt, and the love of my life, to whom I had been married for twenty-two years, left. Everything that I had tried to save, I lost.

At my lowest point, God moved upon a prophet (through a dream) to reach out to me. I had not seen or spoken with this man in over fifteen years. The Lord gave him a very specific vision of His plan to put my life back on track and to restore my ministry. As I began to reach out to God, and He began to realign me with His purpose, doors began to open...doors of which I was not even aware.

My children, who at the time were young adults (late teens and early twenty's), wanted to relocate back to Louisiana. My children and I then moved to New Orleans. I was not particularly a "fan" of the Crescent city, however, little did I know, God had taken me on a journey much like Jonah. He brought me to a wicked city that He wanted to save.

I had no intention of starting a church in New Orleans when we moved there in 2016. I knew that I was deeply damaged from the past eight years and probably years before that. I had never spent any time in New Orleans, other than on the Interstate and in the French Quarter, but now we were living in the heart of Uptown.

God blessed me with a bicycle, and I rode that bike all through town. It gave me a view of the city I had never had before. As I rode through the city, I was able to look into the faces of its people, and a burden began to grow. It wasn't until November 2020 that it hit me...this is where God wanted me to be!

It was Thanksgiving weekend. My kids had gone to North Louisiana to spend the balance of the holiday with their mother and her family. I was alone in the city and, as I rode my bicycle through town, an overwhelming burden came upon me. God showed me that He had brought me through brokenness to the place He wanted me to serve.

So, right in the middle of the Covid pandemic, and after a series of hurricanes that hit the state, we started focusing ministry on the city of New Orleans. Up until that time, I had only felt like God had me there for prayer ministry. But now I see that this was simply the preparation...the opening of the door for me to enter the service.

We were set to start in September 2021, but we were hit by a hurricane and so our ministry shifted to caring for those affected by Hurricane Ida. We distributed over $50,000 worth of air conditioners, generators, diapers, water, food, plastic tarps, and clothing. My children and I did what we could to alleviate the suffering and to connect with people.

On Easter Sunday of 2022, Church of the Apostles New Orleans held its first Service. In attendance was my son, Philip, a couple with their granddaughter, and myself. Since our first service, we have seen one hundred people baptized in Jesus' Name and receive the Holy Ghost.

We have given away tens of thousands of dollars worth of supplies to the homeless. We have seen people brought from living on the street, who now fully support themselves, and are now living for God and contributing to the Kingdom. We are currently working on raising money to create housing for the homeless and for those trying to re-enter society while battling addiction.

We have established two campuses in the New Orleans metro area. One in Uptown New Orleans and the other in Belle Chase, Louisiana. We look forward to God leading many souls into the Kingdom here in New Orleans. To God be the glory!

THIS IS MY STORY

Jeff Ready
Kansas City, Missouri

I was not raised in an Apostolic home. When I got into my early teens, I started using drugs and alcohol. Subsequently, by age thirteen I started selling drugs to keep up with my own habit.

The summer I turned seventeen, some friends and I went swimming at a creek where people often would go to party. There was a county dump nearby where people would shoot target practice at cans and other targets. On this day, six of us were swimming, drinking, and using drugs. We heard shots up the hill. I assumed it was someone shooting at the dump. We went to see who was there, and when we got up the hill, a man was holding two people on the ground with a gun. He was talking to them about something. It didn't look good.

He ended up shooting them both, killing them. He then turned the gun on me, saying, I know the rest of these guys but not you. A mutual friend talked him out of killing me. We spent all summer in court. He had murdered those two people for telling on him, although they had not. Mistaken identity. Later, I found out they were backslidden from a Pentecostal church.

As a child, my parents took me to church, and I had been baptized in my church. But I knew when he pointed that gun at me, if he shoots, I'm lost. This started two things. First, I started questioning everything I had been taught in my parents' church. If "once saved, always saved" was wrong, what else was wrong? If I was lost and what I had been taught was wrong, then what is right? Second, I spiraled downward into heavy alcohol and drug use.

When I graduated from high school, I was out of control. I got a half scholarship to Berkeley College of Music but didn't go. I could go out with friends after work on Thursday, they may have a couple of drinks and go back to work Friday. I would be the one who wouldn't show back up until the next Tuesday, just on a binge.

By nineteen, I had a five-hundred dollar a day addiction: using cocaine, heroin, ecstasy, and all of the other junk that comes with being a "junkie." One other guy, and I, thought we were invincible. We were buying drugs in Houston, Texas, then traveling the Gulf Coast to distribute them. Stopping to party and sell drugs in Lake Charles, Baton Rouge, New Orleans, Biloxi, Gulfport, Mobile, Pensacola, and ending up in Panama City. Thousands of dollars coming in. We were using most of it for our own habits or giving some away at parties to "friends."

I got connected with a man who owned four nightclubs in New Orleans. He was part of the New Orleans mob, crime syndicate. He would let us sell in his nightclubs for a percentage of the profit each night. Through him, I ended up selling cocaine to the mayor of a small city of about thirty-thousand people or so. I literally thought I was invincible.

But inside I was broken. I was angry. I was scared. By twenty years old, I had been a pallbearer in seven funerals: close personal friends whose families asked me to be a part of their funeral. Some auto accident deaths, two overdoses, and one was shot.

There was another extremely traumatic, brutal murder that happened that I still cannot talk about that kind of really scared me and shocked me out of my delusions.

During all of this, I had been invited to an Apostolic church. I started visiting, and one revival night, God filled me with His Spirit, and I was baptized in Jesus' Name! In one night, He delivered me from eight years of addiction. I was free from drugs and alcohol. It took about four months to quit smoking cigarettes, but otherwise, I was completely free. It was a drastic change. In less than a year I was enrolled in Bible college.

One day in prayer God said, tell your story. I said, I don't want to, it's embarrassing. He said, how many people could you help if you told your story. I said, God, I'm trying to tell people "Your" story.

You see, I was trying to use God's story to reach people. But God was wanting to use my story to reach people.

We have served in many ministry capacities. We've planted a church, planted three daughter churches, and started three preaching points on Native Reservations. One thing I've found is that people are hurting. People need to hear your stories. Everyone has hurts, habits and hang-ups, and they need to know they are not alone. Now we get to start churches and recovery programs on Native Reservations all over North America!

Some of the issues we regularly see are rampant drug addiction, 70% alcoholism, trauma, and abuse. 86% of Native women have experienced either physical or personal violent abuse.

But if Jesus will do this for me, He can and will do it for anyone! God is opening some amazing opportunities for us to minister to many people from many different tribes of Native people. To God be all the glory! They need to experience wholeness and freedom found in Jesus. Remember, the gospel is only good news if it gets there in time!

THIS IS MY STORY

Jason Reed
Winchester, Tennessee

I was not raised in any type of church at all. Both of my parents were alcoholics, and I began to be terribly abused at age five. At the age of seven my parents began giving me Xanex and forced me, my siblings, and cousins to fight each other. The loser would suffer more abuse at the hands of the adults.

This continued until thirteen years of age, at which time I packed a bag and left home. I found myself in Chattanooga, Tennessee, homeless until I was fourteen. Someone took me in and taught me how to "cook" and use methamphetamines, which continued for two years.

At sixteen I was sent across state lines to sell meth and then bring the money back. The following year, at seventeen, I was busted in the state of Texas. Police found twenty-nine and a half pounds of meth in my possession, two weapons, and $308,000 in cash.

Because of the amount of methamphetamines in my possession, I was charged federally as an adult. I was sentenced to twenty years in prison and spent time in various federal prisons in a number of states.

During my time in prison, the person who had taken me in at fourteen would send me money and drugs throughout my prison stay. Prison guards would look the other way and allow it to get through to me. I also gained a pen pal, a lady friend, while in prison, and we stayed in touch.

After thirteen years, I was released from federal prison. Upon my release, I married my pen pal, and we bought a house, although unbeknownst to her, I was still in active addiction.

One day, while shut away in the bathroom, I was preparing my drug when my wife opened the bathroom door to find me about to inject myself with meth. She left me.

I was spiraling into more drugs. I was down to one hundred and thirty pounds and looked rough. Then I met another lady, who was also a drug addict. We stayed together for all the wrong reasons. I was in and out of county jails for one reason or another.

In the early part of 2022, I heard about a program to help people with addictions. It was mandated from the county that I enter the program. When I got to the house everyone inside was getting high. I thought, if they're all getting high, they might as well buy it from me, so I contacted my girlfriend, who would bring drugs to me at the house, and I would sell it.

One day the director of the house came and demanded I take a drug test. I refused and left the program. I walked for two days to get away. I eventually turned myself in and spent six months in county jail. After serving the six months, my probation officer asked me what my plan was. I said I didn't know. She told me about a "Faith" based program and told me if I didn't go into it, I would eventually go back to jail.

Just after Christmas of 2022, I entered the R3 Recovery Program in Winchester, Tennessee. When I entered, I found some good guys who seemed to be doing very well. One of the men in the program said to me, "The best advice I can give you is get to know God." I said, "How can I get to know somebody I don't know?"

Wednesday evening, we attended First Apostolic Church of Winchester, Tennessee. People were running in the aisles and worshiping outwardly. I said, "I will not drink the Kool-Aid." Come Sunday, the church had communion. They passed out the small cup of grape juice for communion and again I said, "I will not drink the Kool-Aid." I did not participate in communion that day, but I did feel something was beginning to work inside of me.

With each church service I was becoming "hungrier" to know more. I began going to the altar and asking God, "What do I need to do?" I also began reading my Bible.

I was seeing a therapist, a Christian man, and one day he told me, "The reason you are not growing is because you're holding onto something that you are not forgiving," so I wrote a letter of forgiveness to my mother and dad and put it away.

One evening, at the altar, I prayed and said, "Lord, if this is what I need to do, I surrender." A peace came over me. It felt like God reached down and hugged me. I went to the assistant pastor and told him, "I'm free!" I forgave my parents for the past and haven't thought about it since.

About a month later, at the end of a church service, the altar call was given. I told the Lord, "My vessel is empty, fill me with the Holy Spirit." That night, I received the gift of the Holy Ghost. I wept for three days because I had never felt anything like that before. The feeling I had was unreal. Since that time, I am getting into the Word more.

Through the help and guidance of First Apostolic Church and the R3 Program, I was able to surrender my life to Jesus, and He was able to deliver me from my addictions...they literally saved my life! They loved me for who I was and what I was trying to do for myself. Having their support made it easier for me. I haven't had the taste for drugs since being delivered. God restored my soul.

I've gotten my driver's license back, I'm off probation, and the state has no more hold on me. I am back at work. I had not spoken to my brother in years, but we re-established our relationship.

Thanks to the power of God and R3, I have been Revived, Restored, Recovered!

NOTE:

The R3 Recovery (Revived, Restored, Recovered) Program, which helped Jason overcome, was established in February 2020 as a ministry of the First Apostolic Church in Winchester, Tennessee.

First Apostolic Church had a vision and desire to reach beyond the four walls of the church building to help addicts overcome their addiction by combining resources, spiritual help, and application.

R3 began with a "safe house" for men and, since its inception, has added a safe house for women as well, in mid 2023.

R3 holds two recovery meetings per week as well as providing prayer, guidance, and church services.

It is the goal of First Apostolic Church of Winchester, Tennessee, to assist other churches and ministries in establishing recovery programs in other areas, by way of materials, guidance, and support.

If you, or someone you know and love, are battling the stronghold of addiction, or if you have a ministry you would like to expand into recovery, we encourage you to reach out to the R3 Recovery Ministry at R3recovery2020@gmail. com

THIS IS MY STORY

Joel Revalee
Memphis, Tennessee

I am a scientist. I hold a PhD in Physics from one of the great public universities in the United States – The University of Michigan. When I was applying to graduate schools, they were ranked 12th or 13th overall in my field of study (i.e. Biophysics). A degree from there would carry weight and be a good solid mark on my résumé – and yes, career scientists do certain things to bolster their curriculum vitae.

In my junior and senior years of undergraduate schooling at The University of Memphis, I studied and trained hard to prepare myself for success in graduate school. I spent hours taking practice tests that would help me be ready for the big three-hour exam that all future physics graduate students must take: the GRE Physics subject test – kind of like a final exam, only it covers all the raw material that a Physics student would need to know before entering graduate school. The hard work paid off: I scored in the 95th percentile. My score was 950 out of 990.

Once I arrived in the graduate Physics program,

I worked and performed high-level research for six years in a Biophysics lab. I learned a lot about experimental biophysics and garnered some useful skills for my career ahead. My high GRE Physics score, combined with my 4.0 undergraduate GPA, allowed me to obtain a fellowship that paid my way for the first two years. I applied for and won a National Science Foundation (NSF) Graduate Research Fellowship that paid for the next three years. A teaching assistant-position paid my way in the last year – lots of grading papers, etcetera.

Parallel with all these efforts, I also began training in the ministry. I was often meeting with Bishop Parent in Auburn Hills, MI., discussing the things of the Lord, and talking about revival and different elements of the Word. I had already read the entire Bible through, cover-to-cover, four times. I was now going through a 5th time, more slowly, trying to get as much out of it as I could. In my final months in Michigan, on July 28, 2013, I was ordained in the ministry. That was a good day – a statement that while I was a scientist, I was also a preacher. I was both – in between two worlds, yet at the time I believed that science was still my main calling.

Upon graduating, I knew where I wanted to work: St. Jude Children's Research Hospital. It was in my hometown of Memphis, TN. I was offered jobs by two different principal investigators at St. Jude, and I accepted one in the future department of Cellular and Molecular Biology. Officially, I was a Postdoctoral Research Fellow (or, "Postdoc", for short). I was doing fulfilling work. I enjoyed the prestige of this job. Hopefully, I was building up a curriculum vitae that would allow me a shot at some high-powered professorships in the future. Everything was on track.

But it is in those moments where often our lives can shift. You see, CHANGE is not a scheduled meeting on your google-calendar. CHANGE chooses its own times and places. But this was no ordinary change in my life up ahead – this was God Himself, intervening and shifting the course of everything to come.

Over a number of days and weeks, I began to become dissatisfied – not with science, not with my coworkers, and not even with the work that I had accomplished. I just *felt* that what I was doing was not truly what I should be doing. Unidentified dissatisfaction can be frustrating, so I did what we all should do: I spent time in prayer. Days. Weeks. Hours, praying – asking God what I should be doing? What was wrong? What did He want from me?

I remember the day it hit me. I did not hear choirs of Heavenly singing, or even an audible Divine voice then. I just knew – knew beyond any doubt – that I would be LEAVING my job. Leaving Science. Leaving my career and the future possibilities that it held ahead for me.
- I would not be a professor of Physics.
- I would not be a laboratory scientist.
- I would be a preacher, full-time.

The Lord had allowed me to straddle the fence for years, to do both. To preach as a lay minister and to work in scientific fields. I had attained a license in an Apostolic organization, and so far, being scientist-preacher was good for me. But it wasn't permanent – it was a transitory state. I had to choose. And God made the choice CLEAR for me – He wanted me to commit my life to Him.

What do you do, when you have what you thought you wanted but then realize you are out of the will of God?

I had to choose: would it be God's will, and a future as a preacher? Or would it be "science", and what I thought I had wanted. I wrestled for six to eight months in this condition, but I eventually chose. I resigned my job as a scientist, and I launched out as a full-time traveling minister... and it was the best decision of my life!

Maybe you're reading this, and God is asking something similarly shocking of you. Maybe you think you'll wallow in poverty or languish in the unknown of what lies beyond that next door. But I write this to assure you that the Holy Ghost has your future and potential blessings outstretched. The only act required is one of faith: to believe that it will work out if you do the will of God.

Whether you're called as a missionary, as a soul-winner, an evangelist, prophet, apostle, pastor, or teacher – just trust Him. Maybe you aren't being asked to leave your job, like me – or maybe you are. But whatever His will is for you, God's got this!

Trust in the Lord with all thine heart; and

lean not unto thine own understanding. In all thy ways acknowledge him, and he shall direct thy paths.

Proverbs 3:5-6

Section Three

THIS IS MY STORY AND CLOSING THOUGHTS

THIS IS MY STORY

Elton F. Chesser
Tullahoma, Tennessee

It was just after New Year...a typical freezing, snowy winter in the Chicago area. For some reason our pastor loved having revival services at our church during those January and February winter evenings.

When I say revival, I'm not talking about Saturday night and Sunday morning. Back then, we had revival services from Tuesday night through Sunday morning and Sunday evening, and sometimes for two or three weeks, only taking Monday night off for rest.

I was eleven years old, and our pastor had asked his brother, who was pastoring a church in southern Illinois, to come preach the services. One Sunday night, after another great message, the evangelist gave the altar call (an invitation for those who needed to repent and make things right with the Lord) to come pray.

Initially, I didn't go up front, but I did notice a young man, who was a little older than me, was in the altar with several people around him. My heart went out to him because, in my estimation (and I could have been wrong), he was one of those guys where it seemed things rarely went right for him. I just thought the poor guy needed a break. I made my way to the front to pray for him.

Upon arriving at the altar area, I found it to be crowded with so many people that I didn't have a spot to stand, so I circled around and stepped up onto the platform just in front of him. I was praying so fervently for him, "Lord, bless him! Give him a break, Lord!" when suddenly the Spirit spoke softly (but rather bluntly) to me. "Here you are praying for him, when you don't even have the Holy Ghost yourself!"

So moved in my heart by what I had just heard, I threw my hands high into the air and began to seek the Lord with all my heart. I'll be honest with you; it wasn't an eloquent prayer at all. My prayer was, as I seemed to scream to the Lord, "Jesus, I want you! You are all I want!"

Instantly the Holy Ghost fell upon me, and I began to speak in other tongues as the Holy Ghost spoke through me. Keep in mind, I was eleven years old. I really did not understand how the Holy Ghost worked in people's lives and hearts, although I knew it was real.

I was completely consumed by the Holy Ghost and lost control of my tongue and actions. I began to spin in a circle, something I have not done again since that evening. I did not hear any sound around me, although I could hear myself speaking in a language I did not know.

When I finally came "back down to earth," I felt like I had never felt before in my life. It was incredible, and I was totally overwhelmed by the Spirit. When I opened my eyes, standing directly in front of me was a lady in our church who was known for being an altar worker, who greatly enjoyed praying with people of all ages. I immediately grabbed her with the biggest hug a skinny eleven-year-old could give, and she hugged me back with the tightest hug.

As we embraced, she said in my ear, "You just received something that you will never forget."

She was correct!

Unfortunately, to my knowledge, my friend never received the Holy Ghost or lived for the Lord, although, as long as there's life, there's hope.

As for me, I turned twelve years old that fall, and the weekend of Thanksgiving, I felt a call of God upon my life. I was only twelve, so I knew it would be years before I would begin a ministry, so I dedicated my high school years to learning all I could from the Word of God and even various other religions and faiths.

This is where my pastor and Mother came to be extremely helpful in my growth. My pastor was one of the greatest Bible teachers I've ever heard, so I was blessed to sit under his teaching. As a matter of fact, my first book, "Taking the Kingdom" is dedicated to him for excellence in his teaching ability. He used our mid-week service strictly for Bible teaching.

When I turned sixteen years old, I began to drive and started working a job. I remember times I would get off work, as Thursday night Bible Study was beginning, and I would race to the church to arrive in time to hear his teaching. I watched his teaching style and his illustrations and determined to learn through his example to become an effective teacher.

I had told the Lord I would preach and teach His Word anywhere He would send me, but I would not teach a lie. I expressed to the Lord that I needed Him to show me the exact truth of His Word, so I would know for myself. This is where my mother came to be very helpful.

One day, I told my mother I would like to study other religions and faiths as a comparison to what I had been taught. She was very willing to help as I found other books, guides, and studies. She bought me many materials over my teen years to help me in my endeavor.

After studying teachings of these other religions and doctrines, I was more convinced than ever that there is no way to the Kingdom of God, except through repentance of our sins, being baptized by immersion in the Name of Jesus Christ, and receiving the precious gift of the Holy Ghost.

I graduated high school at seventeen years old and planned to begin Bible college that fall. While visiting relatives in southern middle Tennessee, before heading off to college, my uncle, who pastored a church in the area, asked me to preach that Sunday night. I was thrilled to preach my first actual message in a Sunday service at my uncle's church.

After Bible college, I pastored my first church at twenty-one years old, evangelized for a few years, and pastored an inner-city church in Chicago, before settling into southern middle Tennessee for good.

The uncle I mentioned was Bishop Philip W. Swinford, who founded yet another church at the age of seventy-nine. I was honored to work with him for two and a half years before settling into the church I currently pastor, Apostolic Pentecostal Church of Manchester, Tennessee.

Through the decades, I have suffered some great losses and failures...many times, at my own doing. Stories perhaps for another book or time. But in my lifetime, I have been instantaneously healed a number of times. I have seen drug addicts instantly delivered. I have seen demon-possessed individuals set free by the Name of Jesus and through the power of the Holy Ghost. I have seen folks, drenched deep into the darkness of the world, receive the Holy Ghost and suddenly desire nothing more than to serve the Lord. I have seen instant healings of fever, broken bones, and incurable disease.

It is said that we live by faith and not by sight. Yes, I do believe that. But as a child of the Most High God, I do not only live by faith. The Lord Jesus proves Himself to me every day. When I have been at my most broken, remembering the times God healed my body or spoke to me, has kept me going. To know the power of the Holy Ghost and the life changing effect it has, these are things that cannot be denied.

If you are reading this book and you have lived a wonderfully, victorious life in Christ, all I can say is keep going. It's going to be worth it when we hear the Lamb say, "Well done."

If you are reading this book and you are struggling with life—perhaps some of the same struggles our friends have shared in their stories in this book, or maybe you have simply lost your way—let me encourage you to seek after the Lord. His power is able to strengthen you and lift you up above the cares of life.

Whatever your story is, don't be afraid to share it. It just may be what that one person needs to hear, to encourage him or her to press on.